DECISION

spiritual principles for those who
intend to make a difference

A Handbook by
Jean K. Foster
Writer of the *God-Mind Books*

DECISION

SPIRITUAL PRINCIPLES
FOR THOSE WHO
INTEND TO MAKE A DIFFERENCE

As revealed by the Brotherhood of God
to
Jean K. Foster
Writer of the God-Mind Books

NOTE TO READERS: *Words from the Brotherhood of God are in regular type. Words in italic are those of the writer.*

Copyright 1997 by Jean K. Foster

All rights reserved. No part of this work may be reproduced or transmitted in any form or by any means, electronic or mechanical, including photocopying and recording, or by an information storage and retrieval system, except as may be expressly permitted by the 1976 Copyright Act or in writing by the publisher.

Request for such permission should be addressed to:
TeamUp
Box 1115
Warrensburg, MO 64093
816-747-3569

ISBN # 0-9626366-4-9

SAN: 297-2476

Library of Congress Cataloging-in-Publication Data

Brotherhood of God (Spirit)
   Decision : spiritual principles for those who intend to make a difference / as revealed by the Brotherhood of God to Jean K. Foster.
      p.   cm.
  ISBN 0-9626366-4-9
  1. Spirit writings. I. Foster, Jean K. II. Title.
BF 1301.B72   1997
133.9'3—dc21   96-52082
                                                                CIP

This book is manufactured in the United States of America.
Typography/printing by Blue Dolphin Press, Inc.
Cover Art by John G. Piper.
Distribution by TeamUp.

Spiritual Principles

Foreword vii

About the Cover ix

From the Writer xi

1 The Pure Intelligence Principle 1
   The Truth speaks to all people, but only
   the purely intelligent can put away their
   learned facts and figures in order to receive it.

2 The Patient Teamwork Principle 7
   The ones with patience will do more than
   throw Truth at situations and at goals.
   They will enter into teamwork with the
   Brotherhood of God who will help them
   attain their life's purpose.

3 The Test the Teamwork Principle 15
   Those who put teamwork to the test will
   lead lives of plenty, for they will want for
   nothing. They will create, in harmony with
   God, all that they need, want and desire.

4 The Inner Knowingness Principle 23
   This principle restrains pride and ego and
   puts the individual focus on the God of
   the Universe. Those who hold to the principle
   have the keys to all knowingness.

5 The Receiving/Giving Principle   31
The God of the Universe wants to give all that is Good. One who lives in harmony with this concept has the responsibility of receiving and then giving in a generous manner.

6 The Spiritual Power Principle   37
Those who remember who they are, in reality, use strengths heretofore unknown.

7 The Cause and Effect Principle   43
The choice of God-mind Truth **now** becomes the decision that rules your lifetime.

8 The Tender Presences Principle   51
Tender Presences who hold you safely within the Mind of God point the way to your ultimate joy and happiness.

9 The Releasing Resistance Principle   57
Until the last vestiges of resistance to Truth are met, destroyed and forgotten, your life will not express the Goodness that is your potential.

10 The Mammon or God Principle — Your Choice   63
Those who would grab Truth and shake it for its creative wealth will emanate the Light of Pure Goodness, but those who hesitate, who evaluate and rethink their decision must "perish" (depart the way of Truth).

Glossary   71

Foreword

*From the outreach of the Holy Spirit,
the Brotherhood of God*

TEAM UP! Those words open the idea to people that God is not a far off entity, a greatness that is apart from humankind. "Team up" rouses the whole self, spirit and body, to attain an immediate awareness of our partnership with the God of the Universe.

The God-mind books appear to contradict the Bible, but they do not, in reality. The Bible is filled with gentle Truth that can, if taken decisively, stir the mind and heart to claim what is rightfully theirs—the wonderful, powerful, interactive teamwork of God and man/woman. However, because many read the Bible and pronounce it literal, they become entrenched in a material interpretation, thus limiting the teamwork.

This book will, in the order of your understanding, present principles found in both the Bible and in the God-mind books, principles that will perfect the teamwork between you and all that God IS. The Truth, when taken decisively, will perform in and through you. Put your trust in this message that alerts you—Spirit—to your power as a God partner.

About the Cover

From TeamUp Editor, Carl Foster

IN MARCH 1996, when the idea of DECISION first began to form, Jean asked for guidance from the Brotherhood of God concerning the cover. She received the following message:

"The design of the cover will reveal an energetic suggestion of beings that address the earth plane needs. We suggest a bright glow pressing upon the earth that appears in enhanced beauty—an opalescent kind of light and shadow that appears to the viewer as earth transposed."

For months, nothing came to mind. Finally, just days before the finished manuscript was to go to the printer, an email message came from John G. Piper, an artist, who offered any of his paintings for the cover—if we found any suitable. Jean, via John's web page on the internet, reviewed his works before she found the perfect design for the cover.

The thesis of DECISION is that now is the time to be "One with God." The title of John's artwork? "ONE." Some of our readers may consider this just coincidence. But most readers will accept the matching of the artwork with the book to be routine when you are in a Divine Partnership with the God of the Universe.

About the Artist

John Ganymedes Piper is a professional artist who endeavors to meld the spiritual and the material in his paintings and sculptures. The inspiration for the painting used on the cover of DECISION came from his feeling that we are all ONE.

John describes the creation of this painting in this way:

"On a day in which I felt very connected with everything, I asked Spirit to help me relay that feeling on canvas. I started painting, and it flowed out onto the canvas with ultimate ease. In what seemed like no time at all, the painting materialized before me. It's the most 'in the flow' piece of artwork I've ever created, and it is the only painting I have ever painted in one day.

"I hesitate to describe the meaning of this artwork because I think it may mean something slightly different to each person."

Piper's mailing address is: P.O. Box 14018, Columbus, OH 43214, or he may be contacted by email: art@infinet.com. His works of art may be viewed on his Website: http://www.infinet.com/~art. Prints of the painting "One" may also be ordered from the artist.

How I Experience Divine Partnership

From the writer, Jean K. Foster

---

*T*HE BROTHERHOOD *reminds me that Divine Partnership is not a tether; it is combined teamwork. I AM, my spirit self, interacts with those advanced spirits in the Brotherhood of God, those who say they are the outreach of the Holy Spirit, those who help me to center in all that God IS. My inner Self, or Spirit, easily connects with the Mind of God, with the total Good that wants to pour through me. And, this connection to God exists for everyone.*

Those who think they must walk bound to the Partnership are not allowing GOOD/God to flow through them, according to the Brotherhood. My life, and yours, opens to a flow of energy that pours out to us and for us. To think of ourselves as "bound," or "tethered," rejects our teamwork with divine energy. To think in terms of being favored by God or not being favored is another form of rejection. To believe that only a few receive Good upon request is to thwart the flow of energy. To encourage thoughts of our unworthiness or our wrong approach to God further renounces divine energy.

My call to the Brothers, willing and helpful spirit entities who help me center in God-mind Truth, is answered much more quickly than it takes me to write this sentence! "Brothers!" I often say, "What do I need to know and do about this situation?" And, peace comes within me, the peace that passes all understanding. Then I—my spirit self—realign with the Source of all wisdom, all Truth. My breathing slows and I "see" that host of friends who open their minds to me.

What they do is to help me center in all that God IS—without a need to tell God what I want, what solutions are acceptable to me or how to accomplish the outworking of the problem or the achievement of the goal. Divine Partnership is either a total commitment, or else it is a some time thing with very uneven results.

*Zealousness no longer presides in my life, though it once did. Through experimentation in my laboratory (my lifetime), I have learned that I can allow Good, or God, but I cannot **force it**. Intensity no longer rules this house (body self). My commitment to my God Partnership is not passionate; it is calm and restful.*

A professor of a methods course in English education made a great impression on me when I took her class at Indiana University. Her very wide brow was smooth and her mouth often curled into a smile. "Don't frown or yell at your students," she told us. "All you'll get are wrinkles." Indeed, it is true that our responses to occurrences in our lives project

FROM THE WRITER

themselves on and in our body selves and in the world around us.

What I have learned in my laboratory is that I am not a victim of any situation or any person. The Jean Foster personality retreated to allow my spirit Self to converse with God—an exchange that benefits this lifetime, the people around me and the planet itself.

All the God-mind books were written, published and placed on book shelves, according to the Brotherhood, so that they may lead seekers to them. Regularly I receive letters telling of "The God-Mind Connection" falling off shelves at people's feet. One man said he found it at a flea market for a dollar. Some say they pay for the book not even knowing its title, for they know they are to read it.

This most recent book, "DECISION," is a synthesis of the principles explained throughout the two trilogies—"Trilogy of Truth" and "Truth for the New Age." This publication, for those who intend to make a difference, is a handbook that people can carry with them. The Brotherhood insists that the time is **NOW** *for us to use the spiritual principles that will bring this planet into the teamwork of Truth. The warning is not to produce fear, but it is to produce our commitment to God Truth, or principle.*

1

The Pure Intelligence Principle

*The Truth speaks to all people,
but only the purely intelligent can put away
their learned facts to receive it.*

PURE INTELLIGENCE—that awesome cellular knowingness of the vast potential—belongs to you. You, body-spirit, recognize, at least sometimes, that each cell connects its intelligence to the vast wisdom beyond your physical senses. It is this vast wisdom that we speak about here.

When you succumb to this knowingness, you take charge of your body and—without limitations—the world around you. You become a part of the re-creative force that inherits a wealth of resources. You become, because of your inheritance and your acceptance of it, a purely intelligent spiritual/physical being.

A paradox? Yes, appearances suggest that what is said here is incongruous, even inconsistent. The way of reality, however, is not found in conventional wisdom, dear reader. The way of reality lies in the spirit who knows its Power, its Wisdom.

How can we stay unified—spirit with Wisdom? How can we put a unified spirit in charge when appearances seem to belie our power to make use of pure intelligence? Yes, these are the right questions—as far as they go. However, they stop short of asking questions of the infinite energy of the universe, the intelligence born with you. Try another set of questions: Who can give me the answers? Who is the Source? The Wisdom?

Those who team up with you—the Brotherhood of God—give you answers that put you into the midst of teamwork with Wisdom. These advanced spirits, who announce that they are the outreach of the Holy Spirit, derive their greatest pleasure from helping spirit selves in human bodies. It is they who hone your awareness of Wisdom; it is they who quiet your frantic thoughts and connect you to your own cells imbued with Wisdom. It is the Brotherhood of God who opens doors of Wisdom and invites us to enter therein.

As to the question of who is the Source, here is the explanation. The Source of all Good carries no judgment of anyone. That which is Good requires nothing from you — just your acceptance of it. How can that be, you ask? Aren't there undeserving people? The answer is, simply, Universal Good can be tapped into by anyone who seeks Good. There are some who wince, of course. There are others who shake their heads. But, there are many who hurry to take advantage of the offer of Good.

Those who now invite Good to flow through their cells and through their thoughts will manifest Good, or Truth. Spirits in human bodies who invite the ultimate Good—or God—to express through you in this lifetime, conquer your indecisiveness and make an absolute commitment to accepting Good. Make your decision firm. Make it pure in intention. Make it harmonize with the nature of the Truth that promises us that we can claim, and thus have, all that we need and all that we want in the nature of God/Good.

To understand Wisdom is different from making use of it. Therefore, we offer this example: Teaming up with Wisdom is the same as teaming up with energy. The body you live in operates in an energy field that brings in whatever the body needs to be whole. Yet, when the body appears to go awry, do we say the body fails at wholeness? No, we say that the body becomes sick or diseased. In the physical, options insist on medical opinions and treatment. Now think of Wisdom, the energy field from which each cell takes according to its need. Prove in your own physical body that energy positions itself where needed IF you center your Self in the better understanding of Wisdom.

Still wondering? Confused? Then think of Wisdom as your inheritance from the totality of Good. Claim what is yours. Say, or think, "Every cell in my body responds to Wisdom, for that is how cells are made." Your cells remember their inheritance and seek what is pure intelligence. Say, "I am making a decision to allow my body cells to bring in whatever is needed for perfection and wholeness. So be it."

"So be it" resonates with universal energy, and thus you have claimed the energy through the cells' pure intelligence. Prepare now for wellness, for wholeness, for the experience of teamwork.

This Truth wants to be demonstrated: **Pure intelligence lies within us and only waits to be claimed.** Some people back away, afraid of disappointment, perhaps. Others declare their belief in what has been written here. Nevertheless, their lives do not change. Only people who decisively claim the Truth (principle) and demand that it work in their lives will prove our theorem. These are the ones whose cells flood with energy and whose lives, from this moment on, depend on their welcome of pure intelligence operating in their lives.

Now—we invite the reader to establish herself or himself in pure intelligence. Place your entire body/spirit into your inner temple—the place you have created with your divine imagination plus the teamwork with your God Partnership. If you have no inner temple, take time now to build one.

The second of the God-mind books, The Truth That Goes Unclaimed, *describes in some detail the development of an inner temple. Also, there is a whole chapter called "The Temple Builders" which presents many anecdotes about people who built and use their inner temples.*

THE PURE INTELLIGENCE PRINCIPLE

When you believe that you stand or sit within your temple, invite the Law of Wisdom to be brought to you. Then expectantly, without resistance, team up with whatever is made clear to you. Thank your helpers, the Brotherhood, and accept the Truth although you may not fully understand what comes.

Open your eyes at this point to the world around you. With the Truth that you may only partially understand, what can you accomplish in your life? Is it a health situation? Is it a relationship problem? Is your life full of stress? Point the Truth you have now willingly received at whatever comes to your immediate attention.

Write down whatever thoughts come to your mind. Perhaps a God Jar[1] will be useful here. Resonate (relate harmoniously) with the activity we suggest. By connecting Truth (principle) to your goals and problems, you formulate a unified environment of creative intelligence with the earth plane. In other words, you put Truth with your lifetime experiences, and the results are what some people call "miracles." Rely on miracles, for they do not appear as a bonus to a particularly blessed person. They appear to those who claim their Truth and become one with that Truth.

Prepare now to enact the Truth that lies within you. Prepare now to make a decision that will change your life forever, a decision to connect Truth

---

[1] See glossary.

(principle) to your goals and problems. Prepare now to expect marvels in your lifetime experience.

Meditate. Claim your Truth and ask for help in activating it. Visualize the Brotherhood and you opening your heart and mind to all that your Truth means in your life.

Place your standard bearer—your decision to manifest Truth now—within your temple. In your own expression, state your decision clearly; place it in your temple's workroom where you invite the God Presence and the helpers from the Brotherhood of God.

Then add, "So be it."

2

The Patient Teamwork Principle

*The ones with patience in the result will do more
than throw Truth at situations and at goals.
They will enter into teamwork with
the Brotherhood of God who will help them
attain their life's purpose.*

PURSUE NO TEAMWORK other than the teamwork provided by the Holy Spirit—the Brotherhood of God—if you want your lifetime experience to produce positive results. Only the teamwork you experience within your Divine Partnership will establish you within the true pattern you developed before your birth. Your reality, Self or Spirit, entered into the companionship of what people call "God" to make a plan for your lifetime here. When the plan sang with Truth, when it shone with the pure Good of the Universe, you brought it into a human body.

The metaphor of piecing a quilt reinforces what these words mean. When making a quilt, there must be a pattern. The pattern keeps you working toward the one result—an unusual quilt of many colors that brightens home, hearth and heart. There are many, many pieces to the quilt—more than you expected, perhaps, even more than you find the personal energy to produce. You may call upon helpers—friends or family members perhaps—who will throw considerable effort into following the same pattern and helping you achieve your goal.

And so it is with your life, dear reader. The pattern for your life, already established in spirit, must unfold into your human experience, or you are not achieving your potential. Choose this day whom you will serve, the God-mind plan you brought into this life, or a hodgepodge plan advocated by humankind that limits both your abilities and your possibilities. You do not want a plan that depends upon "luck" or "happenstance." Teamwork with those who judge your talents, with those who assess your fortunes, with those who advocate trial and error stalls your lifetime purpose and makes the plan develop the disease of calamitous discouragement.

However, you can call for help from those tender presences from the Brotherhood of God. They will center you in your growth plan, or pattern, and then work to help you develop this pattern into the lifetime experience you planned for yourself before birth. Let us study an example.

When you say, "I want Good to perform in my life that I may be a joyous singer of songs that will speak to hearts and minds everywhere," you speak as one who understands Truth.

Of course, if you have no goal, no awareness of your talents or the plan you want to enact in this lifetime, the fog of unrealized power surrounds you. Speak with authority when you work within your partnership with the total Universal Good. Insipid thoughts involving your weakness or inferiority simply will not do! Power is the knowingness that you are One with God/Good.

Therefore, choose now which role you want to accept in this lifetime. Do you choose a weak role of vague hope and confused thinking? Or, do you choose to be a powerful soul who knows that God/Good flows through you to perform the wonders that are ready to be claimed and enacted?

The key word here is "choose." If we drew up a hierarchy, here it would be:

Be Decisive!
Choose your role!
Value Your Teamwork!
Know your Self as One with God!

These statements, remember, are in a hierarchy—your first step is the last statement listed. It is the primary step in your goal of developing decisiveness. It is your foundation, your positive establishment of who you are.

To prepare for the greatness that is yours to enact, take these steps, beginning at the bottom of the list, and go within. Do not try to swallow them as a whole. Again, like a quilter, you know the picture/pattern you are using will help you in creating the beauty of your intricate design. With the understanding of the "how" and with the "readiness to proceed," any quilter can begin with confidence.

The quilt is a quilt, of course, but it makes a good analogy for our human lifetimes directed by our spirits who are one with God/Good. No, there is no pattern presented to you. Nor is there a catalog from which you can choose. The life you want to live must be visualized within your mind/temple. What do **you** see? What do **you** want?

The three steps to a decisive lifetime totally teamed up with powerful Good are: First, **know that you are one with Good/God.** Know it as you know what color your hair is. It is a simple perception once you quit wrestling with its Truth. Accept it as you once, as a child, accepted your parents' love and support. Failing such nurturing when you were a child, know your oneness with God because in your heart/mind you have always perceived great Good that you wanted to call into your life. That desire came because you have always been One-with-God.

The second step, **valuing your teamwork**, always keeps you open to the assistance of the tender presences from the Holy Spirit. People who trust in luck or who endlessly gather advice from others do not know the way of least resistance, the way to spiritual power. The least resistant way means you are enacting your oneness with God. Open your heart, reader, and allow the Brotherhood of God, the entrepreneurs of spirit, to help you in your lifetime goals.

The third step is, of course, **choose your role**. No one accidently enters his or her life's role! Everyone makes choices, and the choices lead to the role you develop and live out. If you cannot accept this understanding of your own responsibility for your present life, read again about the Intelligence Principle at the beginning of this book. After you have done that, decide how you can change your negative, undesirable role.

Portray in your divinely appointed imagination the lifetime you want to have. Leave out all the "if's" and the "however's." Paint the lifetime you dearly want to live. You cannot do this, you say? You cannot expect such a fantasy to develop? The fantasy, or dream of your heart, will come into being because it is universal law that such dreams will form and become your experience. What about reality, you may ask. We must live in reality! Where is reality? What is reality?

"Reality" is energy—not material substance! And until humankind develops this perception of reality, people will choose to live in a hostile environment where expectations will always be low or even non-existent! We who are One-with-God/Good value our teamwork with all Universal Good. We choose this day whom we will serve—reality in the form of energy available to all or materialism that is gained by the sweat of the brow and which loses its luster.

In Joshua 24 we read, "Choose this day whom you will serve . . . but as for me and my house, we will serve the Lord." According to the Brotherhood, "Lord means the Law." Therefore, we choose spiritual law over the weaker truths of earth-mind.

As you have considered the steps toward decisive living, and as you have worked through each in mind/spirit, you will naturally be decisive. You know, like you know the back of your hand, that you are One-with-God. You value your teamwork with the Holy Spirit, the tender presences or Brotherhood of God, and you have chosen your role for this lifetime experience. You take the idea of greatness into your mind and together with Universal Good, you manifest it in the here and now.

The point made by this principle is clear, we think. Always people have been exhorted to choose God, and now we leave the exhortations behind us in favor of new enlightenment. The choice for God/Good will protect your plan that your soul wants to manifest in this lifetime. No one presses you to live a successful lifetime. The power of accomplishment lies within you.

No one bombards you with anxiety-producing fear thoughts of punishment or damnation! You come into this lifetime deliberately full of awareness of your choice of parents and circumstances. Why battle your own choice? Why construct a scenario that is blatantly untrue—that you were a victim of your parents' lust?

Take charge of the beautiful pattern you designed before birth. Claim as the one with God you truly are. The opportunity lies there—your opportunity to **overcome** and your opportunity to **become**. Decide now which you will choose, the gods and demons of earth-mind truth or the Truth of God that lights your way and urges you forward in a path of goodness.

Prepare a pattern that you earnestly believe must be yours. Trust your inner Self to connect with this pattern. Write it out and keep it where you can glance at it often. Unite the pattern with your powerful thought, and ask for help from the Brotherhood in accomplishing the pattern.

You cannot fail if you gently open your mind to this process and gently prepare yourself to be that person you designed before your birth. Godness, or Goodness, is your reality if you will only **choose and decide now.**

3

The Test the Teamwork Principle

*Those who put teamwork to the test
will lead lives of plenty, for they will want for nothing.
They will create, in harmony with God,
all that they need, want and desire.*

TAKE THIS PRINCIPLE in bits and pieces. The wealth of material given will tend to overwhelm the reader who wants to grow and graduate into the master that produces, in earth form, whatever is needed and wanted. Separate your earth personality from your spirit Self, for only in the deepest realm of Self can you claim what is given here.

Precious jewels open their essence to you in this chapter on the practical use of teamwork. Think on each jewel and put it within your heart/mind where it will help you recall the Truth of the Universal Wisdom. To ready yourself, meditate in whatever way is most helpful to you.

In case you are not a meditator and know not the value of this exercise, we now produce for you a meditation that anyone can follow.

Step 1: Prepare your body. Put your feet flat on the floor, if you are sitting. Or, if you have chosen a pillow, bend your legs inward into a comfortable position. Put your focus on your back, and keep it straight. Then allow your arms to rest upon your legs.

Step 2: Focus upon your breathing. Take one very deep breath, exhaling to rid your lungs of all impurities. Then establish a breathing rhythm that is all your own. Relax into that rhythm. Know your body is still and relaxed. Do whatever you must to relax your body.

Step 3: Allow whatever comes to come. Do not strain at reaching "something relevant." Just allow your Self to claim relaxation.

Step 4: The body may chafe at sitting still and call to you to enliven things. Quiet the body again and reassure it that all is well and that you request its cooperation. Take charge.

Step 5: There is no meditation goal that can be given to all people. Training the body to relax, to abide by your request for quiet can sometimes be a long process. And, just as though you were training a child to enact some goal, be patient with your body self.

Step 6: If there is success in the fifth step, then you can use whatever comes to you in meditation to open to new experiences or to a deeper quietness. You will begin to perceive, at this point, what you want and need from meditation.

Through meditation, you will attain your primary goal of knowing the Presence of God/Good. This Presence brings you peace of mind, courage to do whatever needs to be done, determination to live your life as a partner, not a petitioner of God. Your awareness of the God Presence may, occasionally, give you cause to weep. You do not weep from grief or sorrow; you weep because you can release your tensions over your relationship with all that we call God.

Praise the release, praise the awareness, praise the peace of mind and the courage. Above all, praise the determination you now have to keep your life centered in this pure energy. Praise is a habit that people need to form if they are to increase the tone and the vibration of all that is Good.

The opposite of "praise" is "condemnation" coupled with disbelief in the permanence of God/Good. Praise overcomes the earth-mind projections that destroy the Good and explode positive energy into a multifaceted negativity that spreads and insidiously destroys the Good. Yes, earth-mind does have that power. As you treat it with praise, the Good that is born within your inner perceptions—and is manifested in your physical earth garden—becomes secure in its material form. However, when you treat it with disrespectful negativity, rust forms, and deterioration gets underway.

Reform your own partnership daily. Never think that finally you have become the pure Good in motion that needs no further growth. Never think that you are unworthy of partnership with the God of the Universe. We speak to you in plain and simple language, reader: **The spirit Self of you came to grow, not to stagnate. Expect to grow daily.**

Expecting to grow will create anticipation within you in every experience of your life. What will you learn here—or there? What new thought will grab hold and become your greater and greater Good? Soon you will come to the point when you see life as the bountiful exploration that it was meant to be!

Teamwork assures you that the journey of life is not a lonely one. Teamwork counsels you in the path of God Truth. Teamwork points you in the path of certain Good, if you will allow that Good to dominate your life. Teamwork touches your life and enhances it, just as an artist retouches a painting and adds tones of light and shadow.

Then, you may ask, why is there sadness? Why grief? Why disappointment? Why does God allow all these and even greater unhappiness? If you ask these questions in your heart of hearts, congratulate yourself! You have come very close to the core problem of the imagined separation between God and men and women.

The flow of creative energy will, if you seek it, flow through you. This energy is yours to use. However, if you perceive the flow of great Good as something given to those who deserve it, you think amiss. If you believe that only certain people will receive God power while others will stand in the wings without believing in their own potential, you will perceive separateness. The God that IS must be the God that you perceive, or you will operate your life from a base of earth-mind misconceptions.

Teamwork provides you with answers to all your deep questions. But, you may wonder, how do I hear the answers? Team up! The answers tremble to come to you. Still your mind. Release your concerns. Meditate upon the peace that God IS. Allow the God Presence to overwhelm you. Then the answers are simply present within you. How does this happen? The process is not easy to explain. Yet, the process is undeniably working, for many, many people find they suddenly and inexplicably "know" whatever it is they need to know. This explanation, if we could give it clearly, would defy earth-mind logic and betray physical laws. Therefore, it's enough to say that spiritual principle does defy logic and will, upon receipt of your request, "give" you inner knowingness.

Remember—the teamwork process stems from the tender outreach of the Holy Spirit, the Spirit that has abided within God spirits since before the formation of this planet. The Holy Spirit, included in the foundation of the earth, perhaps was called "energy." Or, maybe it was called the "Messenger of Truth." There are some who think of the Holy Spirit as the "call of God." Whatever you call it, use its essence. This Spirit, or group of tender presences, work with each person. As people open their minds to these presences, they will provide exactly the help needed in addressing life issues.

There is a need, now, to establish in your mind the fundamentals of the teamwork principle. First, each spirit in a human body is free to call upon the teamwork or to reject it. The help, though filled with tenderness, cannot invade your time/space unless you want it to do so. The rule of teamwork is that the spirit in human form must initiate all requests for help. There is no one and only time when you ask for this help.

Let us explain. Teamwork, by its very nature, is not a sometime thing; it is an all-the-time experience. Teamwork is the individual plus those presences who assist that person throughout his or her the lifetime—morning, noon, and night—and then again in the morning. Each request, and thus each response, must be given by that spirit in a human body.

"Whew!" you may think. "The constancy of my awareness seems prohibitive. How can I think about this teamwork all the time?"

And the answer is: Until you put your Partnership with God first in your life, there will be no way to think of your Self from within this teamwork. Review your priorities. Where is the God of Universal Good as far as your commitment is concerned? When you can answer immediately and affirmatively that the Partnership is first, then living within the teamwork is easy.

Prepare now to live your life the way of ease and joy. You can change your perceptions and your life even if you have, previously, lived your life from the perspective of one tragedy after another. You can even change your perspective of life as subject to luck—which is great when it comes and terrible when it does not.

Nothing rooted in spiritual principle is "too good to be true." That is simply an earth-mind truth based on material appearances. Why deprive your Self from its inheritance of pure Good? Why allow earth-mind sophistication to deny you access to the teamwork of all that God/Good IS?

What remains for you to do? Think it over? Talk it to death? Open to opinions of others? No! What remains is your **DECISION**. Herein lies the proof of your Partnership.

♦ ♦ ♦

A faint sound presses itself upon our minds, and the Brotherhood, ever watchful for our Good, weaves a melodic chant to hasten our decision. "Ah-om; ah-om; prepare now to waken to your Good." The chant grows in fullness with voices from both the female and the male energies, and we who perceive it breathe deeply and inhale the essence of Partnership with God.

4

The Inner Knowingness Principle

*Raising the flag of your inner knowingness
restrains pride and ego and puts
the individual focus on the God of the Universe.
Those who raise this flag hold the keys
to all knowingness.*

WHEN YOU FLY THE FLAG of inner knowingness, you are then separated from earth-mind truth—that often tantalizing statement that sounds wise but leads you astray. Inner knowingness is the assurance that you are one with Universal Good or God. This perfect understanding only comes through your quiet contemplation, your time well-spent with the Holy Spirit, the Brotherhood of God. Periods of quiet and times of meditation will call forth God Wisdom, God Teamwork, God Beauty, God Energy, God Thought. There is no other way save through these periods of meditation to put the knowingness of God within your Self.

The Bible says that the way to understanding is through the words and deeds of people such as the wise men of God spoken about in the Old Testament. The Bible states, too, that understanding comes through the one named Jesus Christ and his disciples. However, we point out to the reader that though Bible stories open the reader to insight, they are not intended to be the only way to God. Jesus opened his arms to all people and wept at the wasteful violence he saw in his land. He spoke in parables to help people receive the God Truth they would need for their own lives. Yet, people repeated his words again and again as if in memorizing them, they, too, would be like the one they called "Christ." Never did Jesus, in that earth life, specify a pattern by which people would be saved. He always pointed within. Then he taught them that what was perfect for him was not perfect for them. He said, "I and the Father are one." However, he said much more than that. He declared that people would and could know this Truth for themselves, that they and God are one.

The people who rewrote the Bible thought there surely had been a mistake. They believed that there must be a hierarchy of our spiritual value—that some are better than others. Therefore, they deleted the words from the text that declared that each person could say, "I and the Father are One."

Look through the New Testament and see how erroneously the writers edited the text. Yet, much of the good news remains. Remember that the one named "Christ" assured people that they might do in this world all that he did and even more. The Truth is plainly stated, yet these words suffer misinterpretation more than any of the others. Where is the Truth, you might wonder. We will tell you that the Truth comes to you from your connection with God, a connection that is never broken, but which is often ignored.

To take Jesus' words as the only Truth is to miss the master's message entirely. To walk behind Jesus is to miss your own path. To quote the words attributed to Jesus as if God was one only with Jesus is to miss your own divinity. Out of the Bible comes much that can open your eyes and open your heart. But if the Bible must be considered the "word of God" without equal understanding of the word within your own spirit Self, then people miss the most valuable part of their lives, their oneness with the God of the Universe.

Tender presences who assist you with your lifetimes wonder how so many can put their own divinity on hold while they worship the erroneous words written, edited, amended, and added to by many, many writers through the ages of the earth. Those who wrote hold no blame, no discredit, for they did what they thought they should do. As for you, beloved, the Brotherhood of God, the master spirits who are the outreach of that spirit called "Holy" or "Celestial" or "Angelic," are here to help you. They will assist you in living this important lifetime that will render earth serenely settled into God Truth—if you will make the decision to commit to your own divinity.

The wonders of heaven are small compared to the wonders you can do on the earth plane as a living spirit in a human body—if you commit to living as a partner of God/Good. Enter now into the house of the Lord, the dwelling of spiritual principle or law, and assume your birthright. You are the pure Truth in action when you live by spiritual principle. When you live by the Truth of others, you are eternally an echo, not a growing spirit.

The scriptures are interesting and helpful when people release them from prescribed revelations made by church leaders. The manner of presenting the scripture as the only word of God, however, assumes that God or Good exists only through interpretation. What are man and woman that they are outside the province of the God of the Universe? The mind/spirit that opens to this kind of nonsense is rebelling against the principle of God as total Good. What piteous people they are who must live within the constraints of a people-made religion! What poorly prepared persons they are who try to live their lives without the goodness of God pouring through them!

The principle of our own divinity insists that you are connected to the God of the Universe. You can collect on this principle or you can forego the blessings of pure Good. It's your choice. It's your decision.

When the uppermost thought in your mind is that you are spirit-one-with-God, then you will truly be living the potential you came to express. When you choose the power of spirit who receives its knowingness directly from God, you will rise with the power of the mighty master who lets no one lead him in paths of disharmony, of unsettled issues, of confrontational and judgmental concerns.

The oneness with God concept allows you to stand in perfect unity with all that is of Good. That unity provides you with the power, the substance, the will needed to raise the law into its perfect manifestation in the earth plane. Here is how this process works: You, the spirit One-with-God, produce in the earth plane whatever is of Good. There is no catch to this statement, and there is no weakness in the operation. There is only the powerful energy of Universal Good at work.

Here is our offer to you: Allow your Self to center on the Good (all of God) with the clear focus of your inner knowingness. Permit this Good to activate through you. Yes, "permit" is the word, for you have the absolute power of denying Good or of permitting this Good. Think—"I AM Spirit—One-with God." Do not try to reason with the thought; Allow it to become whatever it can become **in you**.

When permission is truly given, you will create new order of the materialism in your world. Yes, the elements will bow to your spirit Self and await their orders. We hear you gasp. We see you visibly pull back from such a thought. We see some who ready themselves for the adventure of greatly improving the planet.

Point your thoughts at your task in the earth plane. Yes, you will have inner knowingness about your assignment. You will receive the assurance that God partners always have when they are certain of their purpose and their power.

Here is our pledge to you who seriously consider this offer, those who breathe in this thought of maintaining order over the elements. There is no task too hard for us to achieve. There is no goal that is unattainable when we work together in our powerful spirit Selves. Cast off fear and indecision, the two characteristics of the divine human that cause absorption with the ego. Cast off the lesser truth that humankind insists will bear fruit, and instead, trust the Source of Good that will fill your soul with understanding and power.

Take a project **RIGHT NOW**. Design it as the powerful being that you are. Choose it, take it to your Partnership teamwork, and then open your eyes with expectancy to the attainable result. You will probably say, "A manifestation has occurred." Fine! However, know you are working with spiritual principle, not with unstable, unreliable energy. Principle must enact itself because it is powerful law. You, the catalyst for the work of spiritual principle, are needed if the planet and people will survive the traumatic earth changes and the wasted supply of resources.

The bottom line, as people on earth like to mention, is this: You, the spirit One-with-God must act now. "Now" is the key to spiritual work because there is no time or space in reality. Therefore, all we have in our earth lives is "now." Retreating from "now" puts you into the vast wasteland of the unusable focus of time called "tomorrow." Tender presences from the Brotherhood of God surround you to focus your attention on the "now." Receive their presence and receive their understanding. Then, without hesitation, act.

As each person does her or his project, intention is raised to its highest level. The earth-mind saying that "the road to hell is paved with good intentions" is not Truth. In reality, the road to manifestation is paved with your Good/God intentions. Allow this thought to sink into your inner knowingness. "Intention" precedes the act, whatever it is, because "intention" provides a target for the divine substance. When you, One-with-God, provide the target within your inner knowingness, the pure substance rushes to adhere to it, to change it if wanted, to purify it if needed, to enhance it if opalescence is required. Do you now see with your inner eyes the vast power that you may invoke?

The hour, if you insist on identifying life in terms of time, is **DECISION** time. Catalyst for Good, awake to your purpose here in the earth plane. Awake to your plan made before you were born.

5

The Receiving/Giving Principle

The God of the Universe wants to give all that is Good, and the responsibility of the one who lives in harmony with this concept is to give generously.

PROVE GOD IN YOUR LIFE, prove God in all aspects of the "livingness" you experience. Prove God as the Teammate, not as the powerful entity that drives you forth in the morning to work hard and to experience pain.

When you open your whole being to the above concept of God, you become the generous Giver who understands your role in this lifetime. Now, without further delay, pour your Self into this role as a giver to life. If there is confusion, if there is overwhelming portrayal of unworthiness within you, there can be no generous giving.

Establish your foothold in this Goodness/Godness by turning your total lifetime experience over to your divine Partnership. Know within you that no decision, no act is accomplished without the whole of the Partnership agreeing. And how do you know this, you may ask. You know the Partnership is in agreement when no doubts enter your mind about the rightness of the decision or the act. That which erupts as a brightly lit thought must be the confident projection of the entire Partnership, right?

Though you may, right at this moment, still hesitate, know the hesitation comes from one of two places. It may come from earth-mind truth that insists upon research, a poll of opinions from other people and a waiting period. Or, your hesitation may come because you believe in yourself as a sinner unable to accomplish the ultimate Good, even within your Partnership.

What do you intend? What stand do you want to make? Where do you point? Is God real in your life? Examine your thoughts regarding "God."

Does God loom above you as an entity who observes and judges you? Or, is "God" the ultimate Good available to anyone who asks for it?

Is the God you think of a principle of Pure Good or a mash of confusing definitions given you through other people?

Where is the effortless peace that passeth all understanding? Is it illusive and, perhaps, unattainable energy? Or, is "peace" the effect you receive when you ask for Good?

These and other questions are intended to awaken your mind/spirit to its position here—life in a human body in order to connect with God-mind Truth and to bring that Truth to life in material form.

THE RECEIVING/GIVING PRINCIPLE

If you are ready to begin your powerful Giver-of-Good role, meditate now upon these words. Breathe in the essence of "Giver-of-Good." Say, as you breathe in, "I am a Giver of Good." Your breath goes out, and your givingness is established. Continue to focus on this "Giver-of-Good" role, and breathe it in and out until you know without doubt that God now dwells in Partnership with your spirit/soul.

When you have reached this place of certainty, you may begin to prove the God of your Partnership! Place the certainty on the throne—not your Self. Certainty encompasses faith and trust in the Partnership, and determines the power that enters into the transactions that your Partnership makes.

Do you see "certainty" upon the throne embraced by faith and by trust? They are all aspects of your spirit now truly a Giver of Good.

The Partnership wants to be the pure energy of your life's experience, the pure teamwork that will claim your power to create generous Good. Through your partnership you have the power to install Good in the very earth itself as well as in the evidential material world. Know material as substance that either melds into pure Good or which forms only to decay. This material seen in the earth plane evidences that which cooperates with the Good or that which impounds carnage and disaster. Know the difference and be the curator of the pure Good you understand.

Ply your trade, reader and curator of Good, with the understanding that this material world depends upon **your empowered intelligence**. Where you see an emptiness of pure intelligence operating, whether it be in people or in animals or other life forces, know your responsibility as the projectionist of pure Good. No matter your trade on earth, no matter your day-by-day activities, you, the curator of Good, must enter into the reformation of any impurity and imbue it with your understanding of Truth, or teamwork, of pure intelligent Good.

Why stand amazed at these words? Why blink in the face of such a challenge? You are not told of your power to astonish you or to humble you! No—you are told so that you may enact your true role as the teammate in human form upon whom the future of your planet and its people now depends. Pull from your understanding an empowerment package that only awaits your acceptance of it. Blessed is the one who resurrects hope and certainty in Divine Partnership. This one will receive more Good than can ever be encompassed into our words here.

Before you leave this chapter on receiving and giving, we have even more challenges to present to you. Take time/space here to wait upon the Giver of Good.

A Meditation from the Partner of Us All

Enter your holy of holies, your inner temple where you in spirit meet with Me, the Good or God of Universal Wisdom. We are one here in this perfect setting you have created for our lifetime experience. We open the Wisdom that flows ceaselessly into your pure spirit form. Allow this Good to enter without trying to articulate any thought about it. Be a total receiver.

Know Me as I AM, not as others see Me. Embrace the Me that you feel here. Allow Me into your lifetime experience as the coordinator of the plan you and I made for this lifetime. Put Me into your heart/mind and close the door on earth-mind truth that speculates on this experience.

Quietly, without ceasing, allow Me to permeate your being. Then, when you are fully permeated, certify Self as the Giver of Good in the marketplace of life.

And so it is.

♦ ♦ ♦

The established Good (Go'd) is securely within and ready to be used. Hasten this Good into your work place, into your private human relationships, into your creative impulses. In that way, you become a living prayer, not a sayer of prayers.

Coursing through your body is the blood of your life form. This blood is not your life force, however. Your life force is this God-in-You energy. Without this energy, you are only material form without purpose, without understanding, a life enactment without a role.

That you may view this emptiness for yourself, we recall to you the purposeless lives given over to violence and non-harmonic actions. A nonacceptance of our status as One-with-God always results in a dishonored agreement with the God of Wisdom.

This dishonored agreement results in a wasted lifetime, a wasted opportunity for spiritual growth. Though many call the dishonored agreement by names that tend to exonerate the individual, this spiritual principle, nevertheless, stands as the measure by which we understand our spiritual natures.

Each spirit planned the lifetime ahead, in spite of the appearances from an earth-mind standpoint. The parents chosen, the operating circumstances—these were in the plan. How to overcome such beginnings is the measure of our spirit at work with God in this lifetime.

This understanding does not miss the opportunity for you to help protect a child or help the parents to intervene in the environment. Your mission, if you are drawn to such activities, is to see with right (spiritual) perspective and to work effectively in teamwork with God. Do not abandon your own mission or focus on inferior spiritual aspects of growth such as "karma"—the painful growth of spirit that lasts well into four or five lifetimes or even more.

What is brought to you in this chapter is your best opportunity to be that which you intended to be this lifetime—One-with-God. Into this established Oneness stands the reason for this planet's creation, its continuing place among the planets, its prospects for continuance.

When you make your DECISION concerning your acceptance of the role you deliberately chose before birth, you will be a force for total Good, and your lifetime will blossom and increase.

6

The Spiritual Power Principle

*Those who remember who they are,
in reality, use strengths formerly unknown.*

POURING OVER OLD MANUSCRIPTS provides enlightenment for past events; however, this method will never provide us with insight into who we are. The "who" of our beingness must provide the answer from within, from the very soul or spirit that inhabits the body that lives this life experience.

Here is how we remember; here is how we awaken the powerful entity we truly are: Prove your spiritual reality. Prove that the "who" of you is not your personality, not your education, not your partnership with earth-mind truth. The act of proving will convince you of your perfect alignment with spirit, with power, with the God of the Universe.

Proving your powerful spirit connection to all that God IS cannot be hard for those who are living a human experience! Take each act in your life—the act of breathing, for example—and allow the spirit self its way with your body. Ask that you may receive all benefits from breathing, not a reduced benefit or a foul benefit. Say to your breathing mechanism, "Prove God in my breathing, so that God and I breathe as one." If it is your intention to allow God to be in partnership with you, your breathing will subtly change. You will note the benefits. The proof will be apparent to you.

Know God in all that you do—in what you eat, your digestion, your elimination of waste, in your perfect manifestation of bodily cells! What we say here is not of the mystical supposition—no! It is of the fundamental principle of our oneness with God.

Create a test that will prove the worth of what we say here. The notes you make will create, in you, the certainty of your full partnership with the Source of all Good. When you are certain, place that certainty upon the throne and hold it higher than any touchstone you have ever made use of.

Jean's Test:

There was a time when I addressed my body only when parts of it became painful. My full concentration was on the hurt, the ache, the soreness, the discomfort, the uneasiness of all that is physical. And always the incoming energy helped to dissolve all of the above.

Now, however, I focus on each cell's pure intelligence. I allow, without interference, each cell to be perfect. I give no orders, for what do I know of each cell's excellence? What do I know of its power to call upon and use Divine Wisdom?

Jean Foster is now relieved of the responsibility of her bodily wholeness. The process, which I call into focus, performs within my Partnership with God.

"What if I get sick? What if I do develop aches and pains?" These questions, and others like them, question the Partnership. My role as spirit, one with God, is to stay centered in the Partnership, not to wallow in unfulfilling and unwise earth-mind questions.

Another healthful Partnership benefit is my heightened awareness of what is helpful and good for me. The continuous outpouring of helpful information astounds me sometimes. There will be no book devoted to the healthful material I receive, for each useful piece of information is for ***my individual body self****. You must, if you want it, collect your own helpful insight into what is supportive for your body.*

♦ ♦ ♦

Enter here into the spirit that you are; address your body and restore your cooperative relationship with it. Then, whatever penetrates your cells, whatever puts negative energy into any body part, the Partnership will mend, restore, energize, make pure.

Now then, heed the next section of this chapter on remembering who you are. When you are comfortable with your body under the care and focus of your spirit self, you are ready to give attention to the pattern—the plan that you made with God before your birth, the one that you want to carry out in this life experience. Read what is written here and go forth to restore your full memory, your full Partnership.

Your heart/mind must be attuned to God-mind for the pattern to unfold. Only you, with divine intention, can put the God-mind connection into operation. Only you, with your awareness of oneness with God, can allow your pattern to unfold briskly and completely. Only you, with full intent, can complete the pattern in this lifetime experience.

Begin now to put your inner self, your spirit/mind, into the Good that wants to put your lifetime plan into working order. Express your intention. Enter your inner temple daily. Secure your Self into its place of power. Then test the connection. Put it to work **now** not **later when you think you will understand it better**. Realize your inheritance where you stand, where you pursue your life, where you realize the profits of such wonderful teamwork as that with the tender presences from God whom we call the Brotherhood.

"Seek and you shall find," it is written. We say to you, "Open your eyes now to the wonders of Partnership." Pour all Good/God into your dreams, hopes, ambitions, goals. Establish all in Partnership. Praise the outcome and never sever the relationship with God thinking you have surely had enough Good! Enter into Good that you may be the catalyst for that same Good to go out into the world.

For some people, a notebook might be a source of help. Write down all that you place into your Partnership—your business dealings, the hiring of personnel, the profit intentions. Know the death of earth-mind truth, and note its demise as you deliberately invoke God-mind Truth. All will be plain to you. You will know, when you hold open the door to Wisdom and Help and Power, the way all these work in your life. You will feel joy in living. You will prove the Truth of what we tell you here. You will be a master who knows and uses spiritual principles because these bring ultimate Good and success into all facets of your life.

Come. The teammate that you are now, having followed these suggestions, is that remembered self that you may, for a while, have forgotten. Remembrance is sweet, is it not?

7

The Cause and Effect Principle

*The choice of God-mind Truth
now becomes the decision that rules your lifetime.*

PRICE YOUR CHOICES IN THE MARKETPLACE of life. If the cost is dear, would you truly want to pay it? Think about this question, readers. The open market we speak of teams up with your choices that will either insure your happy progress through life or choices that will inevitably put you in debt to the dictator of worry and compromise. That dictator is the senile truth of earth-mind that insists that materialism be its own reward.

Cast your line into the waters that run inside the pure teamwork of all that God IS—the total Good, the vast potential, the verities of the universe. Pull from this stream the absolute personal teamwork that will operate in your life. Or, do not cast your line therein. Instead, operate your life with the judgments of humankind, the hollow truth that insists that might makes right, that callousness protects you from pain, that energy is limited, that wholeness is dependent upon your genes or control of contagion.

The choice, reader of this material, is yours. Where do you stand right now? Test yourself. At this very moment, can you touch each aspect of your life with pleasure-filled thoughts? Can you prepare a thought-inspired feast of activity and reflection and anticipation that excites you and brings shivers to your body self? Unless your answers to these questions are "yes," you have not teamed up with the divine Truth that wants only to express in your life.

Exasperation has no role here. If the questions exasperate you, if they touch a negative response, you only need to reverse the quiz. Yes, you can ask, "Can I receive help in my personal relationships? My career? My hopes and dreams? My desire to help others?" And always the answer is, "Yes."

"But what do I do first?" you may ask. "I have not only asked, but I have begged. Still I have a miserable life!"

"Take the Good," comes the response from within. "Use it in your life however you wish."

"I cannot rely on your promise, whoever you are. You may just be my EGO." Then the person turns away sorrowfully, unwilling to experiment, to fish in the waters of divine teamwork.

The stalemate persists. The tender presences from the Brotherhood never give up, of course. They whisper to you when you are quiet. They portray helpful scenes in your dreams. They come to you in the night or early in the morning and speak of possibilities, of your potential.

You may ignore all these communications, or you may turn toward them in anticipation of gathering divine wisdom that will change your life forever.

"How do I know these whisperings are from God? I've heard that evil spirits will come if you don't protect yourself. I don't want to leave myself open to an evil spirit!"

There—at last—is a strong request: "I don't want to leave myself open to an evil spirit!" Therefore, may we suggest that when you say such a thing, you mean that you want only God/Good. Think of this.

Invite Good into your life. Pay the price for Good which is, simply, your attention to it. All that God IS—pure Good—wants to express in and through you. Open your mind to this powerful understanding. Allow it to take root within you. Put your mind and your heart into the process, reader. Turn to the Light (enlightenment) and you will receive Light.

Those who persist in hosting what they name "evil spirits, evil thoughts," portray what has come to Light to be driven, gently and without animosity, into the universal recycling process. Therefore, do not greet "evil" with negative or violent reactions. The Light that you focus on such projections will restore your lost memory of the Truth. In that way whatever you may now perceive as "evil," will dissolve. You have given no encouragement to these illusions that you once took for reality, and you have made a home for all that God IS.

Restoration of your Spirit Self as One-with-God/Good is what this message is all about. To think of "evil" as **reality** is to call all illusion *real*. Illusion is the appearance we in the earth plane see, touch and feel. When spirits in human form become mesmerized with appearances, they forget that they are to project the Good or God of the Universe. God-mind Truth projected into the earth plane is our assignment. However, to believe that projected earth-mind truth is real is tantamount to picking out a thought, however ridiculous, and then declaring that it is real. Let us illustrate.

Thoughts pour through those in human form at an unfathomable rate. The best we can do from a human perspective is to let them pass through with little attention. However, we may, if we wish, choose certain ones to claim our attention. In this way, we give power to these thoughts; we allow them prominence. So it is with "evil." We name this, or that, "evil." Then we project it upon our inner screens. The thought resides there in a place of honor while we swill the energy around it and through it. What emerges is the reality that we have created and named "evil."

Since we can create evil, we must understand that we can also dismiss evil. We can join in teamwork with the Brotherhood of God and allow these helpers from God to interact with us.

The moment a request for help comes, we can say to those who come within, "This energy-driven flow of thought pursues my mind/spirit. I hide from my responsibility—which is to take charge as spirit,

One-with-God. It is easier to blame someone else—like powerful spirits that are evil. Why am I powerless to change this pattern?"

The answer is not that you are powerless, of course. You who claim your oneness with the God of the Universe have power to live this earth lifetime in any way you choose! Remember these opportunities, reader:

First, **I AM intertwined with God, the Source of All that IS.** Take this statement of Truth and meditate upon it. Gather it into your heart and mind where you will make use of it in your daily life.

Second, **I can be whatever I want to be.** The catalyst, dear ones, is not the God of the Universe! The catalyst is our self—our spirit—our minds connected to what God IS.

Third, **The One who works totally with me is that God expression known as my Partner.** There is no room in this statement for the negative power called evil. Gather this Truth within your being where it will ferret out all negative thoughts and lead them into the Light. Never fear these thoughts. Know only that they respond to total Good, or God, by fading to nothingness.

The cause and effect theory so often cited in the world operates in spirit, also. The cause of anything that exists always emanates from thought, the building block that, according to spiritual law, portrays itself in the outer or material world. Therefore, when we take a thought of untruth and portray it as truth, we produce the results of that belief. If people agree about a thought, however negative or violent or hostile or ugly, that thought becomes evidenced in the earth plane. And the reverse is true, of course. If people agree about a thought that is positive or peaceful or friendly or beautiful, that thought is evidenced also.

Therefore, **the good news is that cause and effect may change the world for the better!** Do you see this? So what is your obligation as a teammate—one who has chosen the One-with-God path?

Teammates work with the power of God operating in their thoughts. Therefore, they have an advantage over those who simply work from earth-mind truth, the truth of man's consensus opinion. Teammates may work quickly, operating within the power of Good/God.

First, **they know to put the generosity of God into their teamwork.** They do not work from ego nor do they operate their lives to advance personal power.

Second, **whatever is accomplished must be teamed up with the nature of God or there will be no demonstration.** We're talking real power here—not just a manifestation of one's thoughts. Everyone manifests according to thought; but only God partners generate the pure, the tender, the whole, the optimum Good into manifestation.

Third, **letting go of all thought of personal power is needed to perfectly execute the Good into the earth plane.** Permit Self—the eternal you—to make the decision, for this Self knows that you have lived many, many lifetimes. This Self knows you are here to grow and to bring Good into the planet. Self understands how tiny this lifetime is compared to timelessness. Self understands your true goals and will trumpet the wealth of Good through you.

Permit the energy that God IS to flow through you now. **Decide.**

8

The Tender Presences Principle

Tender presences who hold you safely within the Mind of God point the way to your ultimate joy and happiness.

RAISE THE TEAMWORK into its proper understanding. Those who reside in this plane so near to the earth plane have no personal tribute to gather from you. No payment is required! To use our teamwork is the ultimate expectation on our part.

Pursue your life plan without harboring thoughts of our jealousy or our wish to hurt you in any way. Tender presences have graduated from earth-mind, you see. We have no illusions here—only reality! Understand? Gather our meaning into your bosom, into that secret place where we meet together, and we will tell you our reliable word that precedes all acts of Truth manifesting into the earth plane.

We, the reliable teammates, harbor no personal ambitions. We have no expression of personality as you have. We who live and work to the honor of Truth prove this much misunderstood Partnership with God. We who gather in this plane as your assistants, as your teammates, know only one Source for all that IS. That Source is what you call "God" or "Total Good." Put no credence into the words of those who express their Partnership in terms of less than total Good, for they speak amiss.

We never cause you to have a misstep or a hurtful injury or a powerful negative experience! Our Source is the One Total Good for all—you in the earth plane, and we in this next plane of life also. We, in total Partnership with the One and Total Good, deny our intention to be other than helpful to you.

Prove our relationship, we say to you. Prove it by seeking our help. We who are as close as your request never deny help. Enter our fellowship where we can work together on this lifetime experience you chose. We, too, center into this experience that your footsteps will always be true to your path.

Wandering minstrels prepare songs of joy for you. Can you hear the melodies? Put your thoughts on hold; quiet your body; center on your breathing process; gently shift into our tender presence. There they are—the minstrels who play melodies unheard in the earth plane, melodies that stir the spirit and awaken the mind to remember its reason for being and its plan for this life experience.

Touch our heartthrob through the mixing of your heartbeat and our song of triumph—yes triumph over the lesser truth that focuses primarily on materialism. You will feel this heartthrob and sense the electricity in our thought waves that speak one to another too rapidly for the human brain to conceptualize them. Allow us this exchange, this heartthrob that penetrates all that we are—spirit, yes, but also body.

What is possible in one lifetime to the spirit/mind who is subject to this heartthrob? Any good that can be perceived and elevated into the teamwork can be manifested. Why wonder at this? Why insist on clever expressions of like-minded examples? There is no simile that will explain nor any metaphor that will suffice to give you understanding. No! Only your **decision** to employ the teamwork will bring you into perfect understanding. Only your perfect determination about the direction you want to go in this lifetime will surmount your doubts and your inner wanderings away from what God IS.

The **WORD** is simply this: We who say we are your teammates in this lifetime stand ready to help you enact the growth plan made by you before your birth! Where is the generous acceptance of this offer? Where is the readiness to perform according to the **WORD**?

Here are the possibilities. Those who step forward and accept our **WORD** unite earth energy with universal power from the Source of all Good. Name the goal you harbor, the goal that you hold close to your heart and mind. Put it into our Partnership, into our teamwork. Then, without discounting the potential in any way, lead the Good into expression.

Yes, we say **lead**, not follow. Here is the sticking point. Many want to work and live within the teamwork, but they wait to be led, step by step, into each activity. Yes, the writer of this material starts with surprise, for she thought we led her into writing this book. Now she remembers more accurately. "There needs to be a handbook, a synthesis of all the principles. Someone needs to write it," she said to us. Who better than she? Who better qualified? Who more ready physically, mentally and spiritually? Therefore, in response to her leading, we pointed out the obvious to her. Without quavering, she began to write. That is the way we work together, you see. We become as One, for in reality, we all—you, this writer, all people, all spirits everywhere are One!

Name your goal—right now. Now you, too, are openly working with the tender presences! To know you are in tune with us, turn back to the beginning of this chapter and review all points. There is no other person who can say to you, "The Brotherhood tells me that you are working with them." That message is never for another person. It comes only from within you. When you ask another to verify your own God-mind connection, you have expressed doubt and other earth-mind truths.

The **WORD** is what you receive from the Source (total Good) in the exact proportion to your belief and acceptance of that Source working in your life. Will you decide now to accept this principle/law? Will you gather your Good daily and be generous with it? Will you free all dis-ease and cancel all fearful thoughts as they appear? Then you will experience what you came into this lifetime to experience—total Good!

THE TENDER PRESENCES PRINCIPLE

The Tender Presences—those who help you keep your focus on the Source of all Good—ready themselves for an avalanche of requests. Now that you have read this principle and decided to accept it as the law of your life, we know you will want to experience all that you can be and do all that you can do for Good in the earth plane.

Release your hesitancies, beloved. These hesitancies are born of the inferior teamwork with earth-mind that promises you very little of the true rewards of life. Take. Eat from My bread that is broken for you and for many. Know the bread to be My **WORD**, which is scattered (broken) wide through this writer and many, many others.

Open your hearts and minds to ME, the God/Good that wants to be expressed in you, My beloved daughters and sons. What you will receive will taste of sweetness, for the entire universal Good cannot but help you feel the joy of a glorious lifetime. Do not expect pain, dear ones. Expect joy. You draw to you what you expect. Is it not written that you make your own reality? Is it not spoken that what man claims, man also receives? Then choose wisely the expectations you acknowledge, for they will manifest in your life.

Many people seek God. Yes, that is true. However, they also expect pain, disease, suffering of all kinds. Are not these two, the seeking and the expectation, working in opposition? Therefore, know that seeking God is seeking Good to express in your life. Your expectation must be consistent with the seeking! Speak your expectation as envisioning total Good manifesting through you in your life, in your world, and in the lives of others.

Now you see how this teamwork operates, how it releases you to be all that you can possibly be in this lifetime. There is, however, one more **WORD**, and we must insist that you take it within and become one with it in order to claim for yourself all that we have told you.

The potential that you want to be cannot be measured or judged accurately by other people. There will always be some who want to alter your goals. There will be others who take your life apart for analysis. Those who give heed to such purveyors of judgments will experience pain and inner suffering because they value the "good opinions" of people more than they value their God-mind connection. Let us stress that the **WORD** says that each spirit in human form comes to grow, to fully experience an individual growth plan.

If you cannot understand what we tell you, read the above again. There are many who stop short of greatness because they fear bad opinions more than they want to express God in their lives. There is **no sure judgment** from anyone! Therefore, decide now not to seek judgment, not to give judgment any authority over you, and to ride the thought waves with those tender presences who bring you into focus with Universal Good.

The Tender Presences now stand at the alert waiting only for your **DECISION**.

9

The Releasing Resistance Principle

Until the last vestiges of resistance to Truth are met, destroyed and forgotten, your life will not express the Goodness that is your potential.

KNOW YOURSELF CLEARLY AND HONESTLY. Until you have an understanding of just **who** you are and **why** you have come into this lifetime experience, you cannot accept the Truth of your potential. Potential is not madness of the mind; it is the awakened soul's understanding of its purpose.

Pursue understanding. Call for enlightenment. Know the promise of the teamwork principle. Then you will be without resistance to all that God IS in your lifetime experience. Pursue no alternate path to gain security or to attain recognition by your peers. Pursue only the dream of your heart that **you** placed within Self to carry into this lifetime experience. Enter the inner sanctum, the temple where you meet with the Brotherhood of God, those tender presences who stand ready to help you with your life. These who help can steady your eye, your hand, your foot. These who help will retain a focus on your potential, and they will help you to do the same.

Tender presences open your eyes, your mind and heart when you ask that they do so. Call upon them for the focus, the understanding that will create within you all that you came to establish. Call often until you and they work as one continually. Then your days will be full of Wisdom and your nights will call forth wondrous dreams and goals. Life will sing its songs to you, music that puts God promises into harmonic interworking with that which you are.

Disharmony always disturbs the peace needed to co-create with the Truth. Inharmonious tempests of the heart and mind will always rob people of their stability. Therefore, to persist with the wonder and power of God/Good in your efforts, you need to be alert to inharmonious thoughts, feelings, words. These must stand out like red flags to warn you to reestablish your spiritual balance **NOW**.

Yet, we know how easy it is to slip into disharmony! The earth plane often notes that disharmony is the mother of creative change, and people begin to believe it to be THE Truth. However, we say to you, **disharmony never sparks harmony**. Disharmony repels creative Good. Disharmony escalates like a mist or cloud that rises and spreads among people who open their minds to it. Those who take disharmony into their understanding as the way to instigate new Good know nothing of spiritual Truth.

Truth—God-mind, everlasting and creative—finds in you, the reader of these words, either a fertile conduit and manifestor, or Truth finds an infertile field where no Truth can manifest into total Good. Truth searches continually to be expressed, for such is the nature of God. Truth wants to be invited into realization through you. But many stand aside, sorrowfully, for they cannot believe that they are supposed to be the conduits we speak of. For these saddened ones who think that God is neither here nor there, the pursuance of Truth is a vain task for which they are unsuited.

Those whom we have just described are the ones who allow themselves to turn into pillars of salt—recognizable as human beings but not as spirits, One-with-God. These who turn back to the earth- mind truth will be barren of manifested dreams, you see, for they who were to create now only carry the sorrow that material absorption always brings. They who were born to create Good have lost their way in the desert of ideas and concepts of humankind. Thus, their dreams perish within them.

However, you need not become a pillar of salt. You have a choice. You can learn by way of teamwork how to spread the creative God Truth over you like a blanket. Here is one such God Truth that will help you to build a spiritual perspective of your life: You—only you—build your own world and the world around you, not other people.

Place no stock in the earth-mind wisdom that denounces others who cause destruction and violence, for within your condemnation lie the seeds of even greater disorder and devastation. It works this way. Negative energy dissolves because you allow peaceful, rebuilding, gentle thoughts to prevail, or else it escalates because of your own inner turmoil and violent acts.

Place your eternal gold (your God-mind Truth) on those goals and dreams of your heart. This coin of the spiritual realm will provide you with the means to bring these dreams into creation. Again, it is your choice, your decision to use this golden Truth or to abandon God-mind in favor of earth-mind.

Whom will you follow? The charismatic speaker who calls forth philosophies of the past? The person who analyzes and re-analyzes the happenings of governments and of business and society? You must—if you are committed to Truth, to God/Good and to manifestation of all that is pure intelligence—heed only the voice within. **There is no voice other than the inner voice that will lead you into your potential.**

Free yourself from the belief in mighty government, or mighty economics, or the earth-mind certainties of limitation and lack. How? Take what we say here and initiate the principles as the guidelines for your existence here in the earth plane. As it is in heaven (our highest spiritual beliefs), so shall it be on earth! And so it is, beloved. That you may see this dream within this generation, come to terms with your potential. For it is your potential realized that opens the earth plane to its dream of heaven on earth.

Accept the validity of your tutor within, your spirit self who is One-with-God, who will, with your permission, overlay your life with God-mind Truth just for you. This simple statement encompasses all the Truth there is, beloved. Play upon this Truth with your thought, your attention, and with your actions. Cancel your doubts about the voice within. Realize that the Good you hear is what your soul wants to manifest in this lifetime. Know, too, that to lift these blessed thoughts into the realm of idle dreams or of EGO expressing in a self-serving way is tantamount to turning your back upon Divine Truth.

To turn your back on Divine Truth is to invite the "pillar of salt" phenomenon to express in you. You will talk like a spirit in a human body, you will look like a spirit in a human body, but you will only be a facade of salt—bitter and barren. Decide this day whom you will serve—God or mammon—God or earth-mind wisdom.

"Create within me a clean spirit, oh God!" You have seen it written thus, have you not? "Clean" resonates within us as pure, does it not? "Clean" refers to the spirit that heeds only God-mind Truth, only the co-creative teamwork of the Partnership with God. "Clean" is not a plea to God. It is written to remind people who they are—spirit, One-with-God. "Clean" is not written to focus people on their sins and thus give them power. No! "Clean" never was meant to exhort people to center on their "evil-doing." "Clean" was meant to restore people to their understanding that they are teammates of all that God Is.

"Perform miracles," Jesus said to people, "in the tradition of our fathers and their fathers, for no man or woman can do otherwise with the power (understanding) of God within them." Yes, Jesus told people this when he lived his historical lifetime. Others who came before Jesus said the same.

Therefore, we, the Brotherhood of God who have within our group the spirits of those who enacted wonder-filled lifetimes, say to you, "BE. You are spirit, after all, not a human being who has forgotten life's purpose." Those who understand what we say here will become our miracle workers on planet earth. And, to those who already have this understanding, we remind you to exercise your power day and night. People with understanding no longer stand among the herd of those who await a leader; they stand as wells in the desert, as lights in the darkness, as catalysts of all that God can be on earth.

10

The Mammon or God Principle—Your Choice

*Those who would grab Truth
and shake it for its creative wealth
will emanate the Light of Pure Goodness,
but those who hesitate, who evaluate
and rethink their decision,
must "perish" (depart the way of Truth).*

RESTORATION OF POWER—that's what this principle is all about. The earth plane feeds upon earth-mind wisdom; celebrations are practiced in honor of earth-mind understandings. Yet no parade, no party is staged to give witness to the unparalleled Truth that pours into the earth plane **simply upon request!** Would a parade help people gain Wisdom? Would a celebration comfort them about the "way the world is going?" Would people step forward to participate in this parade or the celebration? Would they honor the occasion by proving to others that God-mind

Truth indeed manifests when we harbor the understanding within us?

These many questions are written here to awaken your understanding, not to tickle your intellect. Intellect merely asserts a method that lets us view what we call facts. These so-called facts change at a rate that cannot be pondered. Facts vary—even about the same subject. Once it was a fact that the earth is flat. Anyone who opposed that "fact" was considered a fool.

To rely on facts is to honor illusion. Also, to honor illusion, we must abandon our inner spirit selves who connect easily to the greatness that we name God. There is **no** way to honor God-mind Truth and to honor earth-mind truth simultaneously. We must, if we would become our potential, forsake earth-mind and go completely and absolutely into God-mind. The nemesis of this choice is ourself, not humankind, not God. People—most of them anyway—believe that if we choose God-mind Truth as a way of life, we will be punished by our peers who will view us as mixed up, or even crazy. And, if we abandon God-mind Truth for the popular earth-mind truth, we can expect our lives to bring us dissatisfaction. Either way, as we judge our choices, we lose.

Therefore, we stay unconfirmed in the divine teamwork, even as we long for proof of God, proof of teamwork, proof that spiritual law works to create our potential. In that "place" of our own making, we betray our soul's longing. "Only the blessed ones— Jesus, Mary, the saints and the prophets could express God," we declare, thus resigning our opportunity to sing our own God song clearly and in harmony with all Good.

To lust for Good—is this the answer? To put our passion in the place of our thought process? Will such intense concentration bring God/Good into place? The answer is "no." Intense preoccupation with any facet of life or spirit prohibits the Good, for fervor constructs its own position in our lives and shuts out all else, including the very Good/God we seek.

Teamwork with those presences who stand nearby to help us is the only way to keep our passions in check. Teamwork is the only way to hold our focus on all that is of God. Therefore, do not allow charismatic speakers or personalities to replace teamwork. Those who ride the waves of spiritual fervor construct a way of believing and living that you will want to emulate. Emulation is never a spiritual path, beloved. **To emulate anyone is to reside in the earth plane as a reflection, not a unique God soul.**

Pardon all who give you their criticisms. Overlook those who shout their opinions and try to drown out your message. Sever relationships with those who cannot accept you as honorable, for they seek to drag you into their personal hell. Pursue the path that you perceive by way of your teamwork that reflects your soul's choices. Make use of help from those who always stand nearby in the next plane of life. In this way you will stand as a rock stands when the storms unleash their fury.

DECISION

Unite body, mind, spirit into One, not three separate entities. In this way you will enhance your lifetime experience. Overcome tendencies to grieve over death, for grief only reflects the teamwork with earth-mind that pours affection upon the body, forgetting the mind/spirit. See one another in the reality of spirit, not in the illusion of material bodies. Know that Good, and know that Love—will endure. Whatever endures is **REAL**. Whatever passes away from view is only material, subject to what we call death.

Not easy, you say? You want happiness, joy, total peace? Only through teamwork with the Brotherhood of God—who long to enlighten you, body and soul—will you find peace. "Easy" life is God-centered, not materially centered. To learn and to practice this understanding is the reason for each lifetime experience, is it not?

Release—right now—ceaseless parades of doubts and anxieties. You need not be a victim to these. You need not entertain them and pore over them. They are not your gospel, are they? Then release them all. There is a recycling service within the Brotherhood that will receive all that you release and recycle it into pure energy. There! Make use of this service.

Realign your priorities. What will you put first? Unless you put your connection to God-mind first, you begin now to erode what you have studied here. The connection to God is your inheritance, but you can choose to waste it, or you can choose to make use of it. Only through this connection can you create the divine song your lifetime is meant to sing.

Take the gifts of God/Good without thought of payment, without thought of deserving them. These divine gifts permeate the very air you breathe, but if you do not allow them place in your heart/mind, they never take root. Say to God, "I need courage." Or, "I need more physical energy." Or, "Grant me your spirit of tenderness, the essence of love." Or, you may ask that you attract prosperity. The possibilities are endless. The gifts will come into you for you to make use of, not for you to wonder about or to ask proof of.

You, dear reader, are the catalyst—the one who makes these things happen in your life. God responds; you seek and use of whatever comes to you. If you only bask in the understanding just given you, the gifts fade from under use. There is no such thing as "over use," beloved, for the more you make use of God gifts, the more they proliferate.

Rise, take up your pallet and walk. This metaphor stands today as it has through all the ages as the empowerment of the individual who understands God Truth. The Truth is the Truth, beloved. You came into this lifetime experience to make use of it.

There is no place in this lifetime where you can learn the ultimate Truth—no central spiritual disbursement center. Money will not make it possible for you to reach the far off Himalayas that guard the secret messages that will empower you. No person, however brilliant, however sainted, can pour into you the God Truth that will benefit your lifetime. You have access to the Way, the Ultimate Truth, the Path to Fulfillment of Your Potential. That Truth is your key to ultimate joy and happiness. The question is, will you use the key?

The teamwork will not lead you by the nose; it will not push you, either. But if you request it, we who stand at the ready will do all that we can to communicate with you, to be with you as you meditate, set your goals, ask your questions, and ponder your next step.

Know us as friends, as partners in your lifetime experience, as waysharers. (Waysharers are entities who helpfully share our life's path.) Proceed gently, beloved, with assurance in our teamwork. If you must think it over, or question others as to their opinions, or enter into rigid study of endless spiritual materials, you will be quitting the field. Yes, if you continue to ponder over your decision, you will sit on the perimeter of your life always wondering what might have been.

Choose this day whom you will serve—God or mammon; teamwork or EGO; acceptance of your personal Truth or acceptance of the truth of others; pure intelligence or the limited wisdom of science.

Those who now accept the challenge from the Holy Spirit, the Brotherhood of God, will make miracles commonplace. They will restore balance to the earth, and they will enter into partnership with All that IS. Yes, there will be great spiritual understanding—a new heaven—and, therefore, a new earth. A mastery of these spiritual principles will extend the parameters of life as you know it on earth. In Truth, no earth-mind limitation will stand, for the new understandings will allow no ceiling or walls.

Respond to your inner urging to align your Self with its plan to become its potential in this lifetime. There will be no greater pathway to tread, nor any life more joyful than this one. Prepare no sacrifice, beloved. Only open your mind and heart to all that your life can be. God demands nothing from you. God stands as the Truth, the seamless cloth that can cover you with protection, the resonating power that will call forth your potential.

Glossary

Bible: A collection of stories, history and remembrances that gives the progression of thought about God. It is a guide for living, divinely inspired, but it is not the only word of God. The word of God comes to each individual as a flow of wisdom, and the Bible, at best, is but one source of wisdom. God, a living, pulsating, vibrant energy, is the Source of Pure Truth, not a Bible—any Bible.

Brotherhood of God: Advanced spirits who stay nearby in the next plane of life to enact the work of the Holy Spirit. They are the counselor, the comforter, the teacher who work with those in the earth plane who open their minds to them. These spirits want to help people team up with the God of the Universe to receive eternal and personal truth.

channel: Anyone can be a channel through which the Mind of God pours individual and eternal truth. Also, an individual who is called a channel is only proving that communication is possible between those in the earth plane and those in the next plane of life.

Christ: A concept of oneness with God. Each person can consider himself or herself the Christ in the sense of that oneness. When we acknowledge the Christ, we acknowledge our oneness with God.

demonstration/manifestation: The process of producing your thought into the physical world. Although everyone projects thought into the physical plane, producing great Good, as opposed to one's fears, is predicated upon a person's understanding and application of spiritual principles.

earth-mind: Earth-mind goes no further than man has gone. It proves its beliefs in material substance, historical data, and scientific observations. Earth-mind also embraces religion as a worthy effort to reach God. But God is often demoted to that which holds society together in values, not a personal Entity Whose vastness is yet to be proved in individual lives.

earth-mind truth: The truth that is contemplated by philosophers, by committees, by policies, by consensus, by observation of historical and biological data. None of this truth is absolute; none is perfect. It is simply the best that mankind has developed up to the present.

energy: Innate power that rises from your truth—either God-mind or earth- mind.

eternalization: Refers to the goal or object you visualize along with helpers from the Brotherhood. They and you work with your God Truth to visualize what is needed, what is wanted. Then, the three in one—the Holy Spirit, the spirit of the individual and the power of the God of the Universe—produce any generous and worthy thought into earth substance.

evil: A concept many people hold in mind to explain what they call "evil." This concept of an evil presence within a person diminishes the concept of God by keeping the individual focused on the absence of what God IS.

gentle or tender presences: Spirits work within the Brotherhood/Holy Spirit to reunite your being with God Spirit. With the help of these presences, those in the earth plane can meet every need or concern with positive, perfect understanding. With their counsel, each person can be useful in society and can assist others as well as himself.

God/Good: The word "God" was first written in English as "Go'd"—as a contraction of the word "Good." Therefore we understand that "God" and "Good" are the same.

God Jar: A container used to represent one's Partnership with God in which all manner of concerns or goals are placed. Frequent re-readings of whatever is put inside helps to cement the understanding of one's Partnership with God.

God-mind Truth: The choice of those who are committed to their Partnership with God. This truth comes to each individual from within his or her spirit/mind that connects easily to God wisdom.

God of the Universe: This designation is meant to open your concept of God to the furthest reaches of your mind. The God concept must be expanded if it is to meet your best expectations. The smaller the God concept, the smaller the expectations. Therefore, the Brotherhood tries to help each individual to open his or her mind to all that God IS.

God-Mind: The unrestricted and unlimited Mind that produces a flow of wisdom that anyone can tap into. This truth that flows with a steady impulse wants to connect with individual mind/spirits who reach out to become one with the God of the Universe.

growth: When a person accepts truth and lives it, spiritual growth occurs. Growth becomes a permanent part of the spirit self.

growth plan: Before a soul or spirit enters an infant body within the womb, that entity made a plan to achieve Oneness with God. This plan, true to the nature of what God IS, is a cooperative venture between the God of the Universe and the individual.

Holy Spirit: The Counselors, Comforters, Teachers described and promised by Jesus to help us live life successfully.

inner self: The reality of each person is the inner self or spirit/soul. This inner self has lived many lifetimes and will never die.

GLOSSARY

inner temple: We are encouraged to build an inner temple where we can meet with the Brotherhood of God and with the essence of what God IS. This temple is the cornerstone of our faith in our Partnership with God.

Jesus: The Brother of Brothers who became the outward manifestation of the inner being who lived his life according to his growth plan. Jesus, the historical person, reflected his inner self and enacted his Oneness with God.

knowingness: Learning and resourcefulness that comes from within, from the God-mind connection.

mind/spirit: The mind is separate from the brain. The brain is physical—material; the mind is spiritual. When the term "mind/spirit" is used, it refers to the reality within us—the soul or spirit which is capable, under any and all conditions, of connecting to all that God IS.

next plane of life: The earth plane is where our spirit selves—our souls—express in human form. The next plane of life interpenetrates the earth plane, and it is here that the Brotherhood of God work as the outreach of the Holy Spirit. It is also a place of coming and going—spirits leaving the earth plane and spirits preparing to re-enter life on planet earth.

partnership: When we accept truth from God and decide to live only that truth, we are in partnership with the God of the Universe and with all that God IS—including the Brotherhood of God.

pure intelligence: Belief in each cell's ability to enact its pure, God-given intelligence thus becoming its potential.

reality: Denotes what is purely harmonized with spiritual principle or law. We cannot measure what is real in terms of tangibility nor visibility in the earth plane sense. It is the "real" that produces the tangible, the visible. Even science says all is energy, and when you accept this statement, you are close to your understanding of "reality."

spirit: The entity that opens to the God of the Universe. Your spirit self knows wherein lies its strength and its wisdom. The spirit is not seen in the earth plane, but it resides within the body temple and lives a lifetime experience devoted to its growth. It will never die nor does it destruct.

spiritual law: Any God Truth that operates within the universe as law—as that which must come about.

team up: This is the directive to join with the God of the Universe and the Brotherhood of God.

teamwork: Living our lives with the certain understanding that we have help in achieving our potential. This "help" is spiritual—thus real and powerful.

The God-Mind Books by Jean Foster

The God-Mind Connection: *Revised*

The reader is invited to tap into that which God IS, into Wisdom, into Creative Intelligence. First published in 1987, the revised edition has added *Postcripts*—stories from people who have made their God-mind connections that help them live successful lives. Introduced is the Brotherhood of God, who counsel and comfort. ISBN 0-9626366-2-2, 196 pages, $10.95

Also available in a six-cassette album, 5 1/2 hours, $34.95

The Truth That Goes Unclaimed: *Revised*

This second book in the series outlines steps the reader may take to allow his personal God-mind connection to be a powerful force in his own life. How to clarify goals, form a greater God-image, build an Inner Temple, and experience truth are explained.
ISBN 0-9626366-3-0, 224 pages, $10.95

Eternal Gold

This final book of the trilogy teaches powerful concepts and methods for bringing Good—or God—into a life experience. The reader learns that Eternal Gold is the God truth each one of us may claim and manifest in the earth plane as substance and changed conditions.
ISBN 0-912949-16-3, 143 pages, $8.95

Epilogue

What happens to us when we die? Where do we go? Will God punish us for our wrongdoings? What is heaven like? Will I join my parents or my spouse? All of these questions are answered in the fascinating stories told by departed spirits who have died and left the earth plane.
ISBN 0-912949-18-X, 173 pages, $9.95

New Earth—New Truth

In this first book of the trilogy "Truth for the New Age," the Brotherhood of God, the outreach of the Holy Spirit, reveals—in an astonishing and candid manner—that the New Age is upon us. The Brotherhood awakens the reader to the necessity of putting God-mind truth to work now, not waiting for a time of travail.
ISBN 0-912949-29-5, 195 pages, $9.95

THE GOD-MIND BOOKS

Masters of Greatness

Instruction that started in *New Earth—New Truth* continues in the second book of the New Age trilogy. *Those who accept the message of this book will be masters of greatness, not servants of their fears or their doubts,* is the promise given by the Holy Spirit, the Brotherhood of God, to the reader who makes a commitment to help planet earth renew its purity.

ISBN 0-9626366-0-6, 170 pages, $9.95

Divine Partnership

The third book of this trilogy completes the leadership instruction which began in *New Earth—New Truth* and *Masters of Greatness*. Here the Brotherhood of God tells us that manifestation is no longer a hoped-for miracle from God. "It always occurs when people use the teamwork principle. Gentle presences work with you when you read and study these books."

ISBN 0-9626 366-1-4, 168 pages, $9.95

I AM GOD'S PARTNER

If you are one of those who has asked, "How do I teach my children (or grandchildren) spiritual concepts?" then you will want to include *I AM GOD'S PARTNER* among your child's many activity books.

20 pages, 8 1/2 x 11, $2.95

The God-Mind Tapes

Taking Charge of Your Life

Jean presents a number of principles outlined by the Brotherhood of God, the outreach of the Holy Spirit. She also recounts many of the anecdotes told to her by those who have successfully applied these principles and taken charge of their lives. Each side of the cassette concludes with a meditation.

85 minutes of narration, $8.95

Meeting the Helpers

Jean discusses "The Teamwork Process—Allowing the Flow of God to bring Good into Your Life." The Brotherhood of God has defined teamwork as the basic strength of the work of spirit. There can be no accomplishment of permanent value without teamwork with your God Partner. In the second half of the tape, Jean presents a message "Preparing Your Life's Agenda"—a guide to organizing your life with the help of your God Partner. It concludes with a meditation.

90 minutes of narration, $8.95

Tenderness—A Key to Joy & Peace

To open our minds and hearts to God Gifts, the Brotherhood of God advises us to let go of old concepts and beliefs concerning reality and spiritual beliefs. Based on the two trilogies written through Jean and inspired by the Brotherhood, Jean outlines God-mind principles that can empower us to demonstrate Good in our lives.

The Universal cry for love and personal understanding need not go unmet for we, the catalysts of all Good, may call for the essence of love and receive it in abundance.

90 minutes of narration, $8.95

Divine Partnership

In this seminar presentation, Jean describes the enriching relationship everyone can have with the Brotherhood of God—our reliable spirit helpers. She explains how our divine partnership helps us to hear God-mind truth and manifest our needs and desires.

50 minutes of narration, $4.95

TeamUp
Box 1115, Warrensburg, MO 64093
(816) 747-3569